Chapter 23

Cheyenne Pajardo

I am *otterly* grateful that you believed in me enough to publish a collection
of poetry.
"May the greatest live forever."

~chicken nugget

I.

Allow yourself the opportunity to try & get it right.

You deserve everything your heart desires.

II.

Perhaps it wasn't that he didn't love you,

but rather he didn't know the way you

needed to be loved…

III.

& just like a flower needs love & sun to grow,

so does your mind & soul.

IV.

May you never wake up & wish you had…

V.

You will be okay.

You will get over it.

You will move on.

VI.

No matter how much my mind says to hate you,

my heart whispers, "don't, not yet."

VII.

The beauty is in finding strength to push on

when your heart tugs to stay cemented.

VIII.

Because maybe not everything is meant to be understood,

but sometimes just felt.

IX.

& just as the sun feels tired & asks for a break, so can your heart.

X.

A break does not make you weak;

it makes you human.

XI.

I asked the moon to dance,

& she whispered into the night,

"only if you stay until the sun wakes to join us…"

XII.

I chose you & your lips agreed,

but your everything else said nothing...

XIII.

Life will test you.

You may fail.

But at least you tried.

XIV.

I thought I needed you like a fish needs water…

turns out I knew how to breathe without your oxygen all along.

XV.

We were two sentences written together,

but belonging to different chapters.

XVI.

I wanted so much to feel needed

that I ignored my voice when it

whispered, "I need you…"

XVII.

Be gentle. Most are still healing.

XVIII.

Silly girl, his silence was a simple "fuck you."

XIX.

I thought I couldn't live a day without you…

then tomorrow became today,

& I was still breathing my own air.

XX.

Sometimes I don't know.

& that's okay.

XXI.

I believe in promises.

The problem is you think you do too…

XXII.

Who says you can't?

XXIII.

We are more than friends, but less than lovers…

somewhere in the sea of in-betweens…

XXIV.

He asked me what I wanted from life & I skipped no beat.

"Happiness."

"What is that?" he asked.

My lips parted & whispered, "When you feel it, you'll know…"

XXV.

Because maybe I didn't love you at all.

But I loved the me who grew from the pain

of knowing you.

XXVI.

You asked me to trust you, so I did.

Why did that mean I had to lose you?

XXVII.

You'll leave just like the rest…

or maybe you'll stay & I'll leave this time.

Because I've finally allowed myself to love again…

love me.

XXVIII.

What's good for you isn't always what's best for you.

What's bad for you isn't always what's worst for you.

XXIX.

Your mouth tells me you're okay,

but the blue in your eyes screams silently.

XXX.

Like the ocean, the feels come in waves...

crashing, one never like the last...

keep up with the rip tide.

XXXI.

I learned how to drive with one hand so my other could hold yours.

I wish I would've known that your fingers were

Going to burn.

XXXII.

You always said transformation takes time.

I guess that's why your wings know how to block the darkness.

XXXIII.

One day I will wake up next to you

& thank God for sparing my heart

all those times before...

XXXIV.

They called me a work of art,

but shuttered when the darkness consumed the canvass.

They weren't art connoisseurs at all...

merely amateurs unable to distinguish

an original from a duplicate.

XXXV.

I wanted growth without experiencing pain,

but even flowers whine when leaves are cut.

XXXVI.

I reached for the phone to call you…

just to hear your voice…

to laugh at the sound of your laugh…

to smile at your words…

but heaven doesn't have cell towers yet.

Can we try snail mail instead?

XXXVII.

I want so much to make my art beautiful

that I forget the beauty in art is

the imperfections & flaws.

XXXVIII.

Dear self.

Trust that you are moving in accordance to your destiny.

XXXIX.

You don't need them, but you do need you.

Please, be kind.

Be gentle.

Be understanding.

You are irreplaceable.

XL.

How can you expect someone to love you

when you've yet to love yourself?

XLI.

Do you just love yourself or are you also in love with yourself?

XLII.

I want to fly, but they tell me I need wings.

How silly are they for not knowing

God's angels walk among them?

XLIII.

I saw two people fall in love inside Barnes & Noble.

Their souls touched each other for a second briefer than 60.

I hope they find each other again.

XLIV.

A phoenix is born & dies from ashes.

Why would you attempt to control the fires within you?

XLV.

You cannot force it.

XLVI.

I wanted to make you feel the way I do

when the ocean waves touch the sand…

you thought they were destructive.

I thought they played music.

XLVII.

I studied you like I would a history exam.

Cramming & memorizing.

Only to have all the information escape my memory

the second my eyes looked at question one.

XLVIII.

I am jealous of the ones you love

because the love they return hurts your

soul.

XLIX.

Feelings demand to be felt,

& so they shall.

Not always rainbows & butterflies,

but the sun still sits in the sky

even when it's grey.

L.

I danced with a 60 year old today.

She reminded me that love does not have to die with age.

LI.

Drugs are illegal.

I guess the toxicity of unsure love

didn't meet the criteria.

LII.

Less stress, more ice cream.

LIII.

You don't like me because I ask you to be the version of yourself

you've tucked away in order to make others comfortable.

Isn't wearing a mask exhausting?

LIV.

your love is not wrong. the receiver is wrong.

LV.

they tell you what it's like to be

in love with someone else,

but never with yourself.

LVI.

I'm so mesmerized by your eyes

that my ears failed me in hearing

the venom in your voice.

LVII.

You love the idea of me, but not me...

if you understood the difference

I wouldn't have to explain myself to you...

LVIII.

"But if I love them, why would I let them go?"

"Because love doesn't convince you you're not enough."

LIX.

I think the worst part about endings

is never knowing when they come.

How could I believe in a forever

when not everything lasts?

LX.

You loved the broken pieces of me

because you thought you could fix them.

Don't you understand creators of art

never make mistakes with their work?

LXI.

Prayers don't fall on deaf ears.

God is everywhere.

LXII.

I have been three different people in my lifetime already.

It's called growth.

LXIII.

It does not take a special person

to understand nor love you.

It takes the right person.

LXIV.

I don't need you to say it back.

I just want you to know I love you.

LXV.

You punish yourself for having feelings that you cannot explain.

You know you're still human, right?

LXVI.

They tell me to live in the moment, so I try.

But how can I smile when I know this will end?

…& I will end up missing this soon?

LXVII.

Every morning I sit at Starbucks, pen in hand, waiting for something
creative & thought provoking to transpire.

Every morning, a couple of friends sit at Starbucks, drinks in hand,
gossiping about work & people.

How intriguing to live in the same space, but in different worlds.

LXVIII.

Goodbyes are hard because most are unexpected.

LXX.

I have never asked for perfect. I have only asked for effort.

LXXI.

I don't write poems about you for you

because you are as undeserving now

as you were when I lent you my heart.

By the way, it's 'Past Due'.

Please return before fees accrue.

LXXII.

I want you to be the book I repeatedly checkout at the library...

the problem is someone else feels that way too...

I'm just waiting for you to return to the shelf.

LXXIII.

The sound of your laugh is ingrained in the canals of my ears.

I look forward to the day I hear it again.

LXXIV.

I'm scared that one day I will forget the sound of your voice & how it makes everything better.

But that's life, isn't it?

Learning to live without someone who gives you light when you're sitting in the dark?

LXXV.

How could you possibly fear life when all your steps have been laid
before you...

LXXVI.

I never knew how much I needed me

until I became the only person I could depend on.

LXXVII.

How can I believe in a forever

when even Disney princess movies end?

LXXVIII.

It's taken me years to tame the darkness that simmers within me.

Please leave the "Do Not Disturb" sign alone.

The door is locked as a precautionary measure.

LXXIX.

I want the 3am French fry run. The parked car conversations.

Talks about goals. Hugs that linger with conversations of their own.

The love that neither of us speak on, but know exists between the two of us.

I want that…with you.

LXXX.

`

How high do I have to jump in order to grab your hand from heaven?

LXXXI.

you do not have expectations. you have standards.

LXXXII.

I almost begin to wonder if you think about me as much as I think about
you...

it's silly, I know, you 'unfriended' me years ago.

LXXXIII.

We often hate the ones who bring rain into our space.

& yet we still learn to dance.

LXXXIV.

Can't we just agree that we should be?

LXXXV.

So often when I find my peace, you come back knocking.

There is a reason I left you on the porch this time.

LXXXVI.

Don't you understand?

The electricity between our fingertips

tells you everything my mouth cannot.

LXXXVII.

I thought I knew you as well as I know the days of the week.

Today is Wednesday. So, tomorrow would be…

LXXXVIII.

You are never too old

to run through the sprinklers,

eyes closed,

arms flailing.

You grow old in age,

but never in heart.

LXXXIX.

I didn't ask you for something as unobtainable as perfection.

I asked you to try, & you turned an anthill into a mountain.

XC.

You did not break my heart.

I broke it myself believing you were someone better.

XCI.

I remember everything…& that is the problem.

XCII.

I felt that I couldn't more times than I felt I could.

But what I felt & what I did were two different things.

XCIII.

We did not speak the same language

& yet our hearts connected when our eyes met.

Funny how souls communicate.

XCIV.

I have a grandmother whose love spans from Japan to America.

I now know love in two different languages.

XCV.

I drove to our spot alone last night. I knew you wouldn't be there, but the air still smelled like you.

In a different lifetime, we are each other's. I look forward to meeting you again.

XCVI.

Do not give me the world.

She's already taken by billions.

Give me a planet less loved.

I'll unmask her beauty & watch her flourish.

XCVII.

Don't you understand?

I don't need you.

I just want you.

XCVIII.

We have destroyed earth & mocked her beauty.

& yet we continue to ask her for more

when she's already pouring from an empty cup.

XCIX.

& in the end, it was a matter of who could

run alongside me without tripping over their laces.

C.

I wonder if you'll be another chapter I tell my daughter about when she's crying over a stupid boy who broke her beautiful heart.

Maybe I'll reference you so she sees that heartache & little boys eventually pass.

CI.

More than half the things we feel or say have already been said & felt.

Do you still think we're that different after all?

CII.

You cannot repay me for the love I give you for free.

CIII.

If you cannot see the light, make it yourself.

Chapter 23

CIV.

I saw a tiny human in a princess dress pretending to save people from a monster.

When did we stop believing in magic?

CV.

I saw no stars tonight…but then I caught your eyes

& watched them light the sky.

CVI.

We collect memories knowing they will one day evaporate.

CVII.

How many firsts will I have to go through

before I find my first that is also my last?

CVIII.

I can explain almost everything to you…

everything except my soul.

CIX.

I do not want you to be my other half.

I want you to be my other full.

What good are we to each other

if we are only half the persons we can be?

CX.

You may not know this version of me.

The pieces are rearranged.

CXI.

I want to believe in humanity,

but my 'News' notification goes off every 2 minutes

ensuring I recount the number of lives

we just lost.

CXII.

I saw a sunflower today.

A small sunshine for my pocket.

CXIII.

You ask why I cry so often.

My heart feels the height of heaven

& the fires of hell

simultaneously.

CXIV.

I keep you at a distance so that my words can continue to pour from my fingertips.

CXV.

I don't want you to think I'm annoying.

So instead of calling, I listen to your voice through speakers to fall asleep.

CXVI.

Do not clip your wings for those unwilling to watch you soar.

CXVII.

You ask me if I hate you.

I wish the answer was yes.

It'd be much easier on my heart.

CXVIII.

I wander back to you when I don't understand the dimensions of love.

CXIX.

Could you imagine what you'd do

if you stopped being so mean to yourself?

CXX.

We think we are born to fix the entirety of the world,

not realizing there's an entire kingdom within us.

CXXI.

You are not broken.

You have never been broken.

CXXII.

Maybe we didn't work in this storyline, but we do in another.

CXXIII.

I dream of packing myself up & exploring.

There are at least 194 other countries I haven't wandered through.

CXXIV.

They say eyes are windows to the soul.

I wonder how true that is.

CXXV.

I am selfish, yes.

Because I need time to mend the pieces of me

all the ones before you bruised.

CXXVI.

I am a woman....

& for whatever reason that seems

to terrify men…

only they're not men,

but little boys playing dress up

in button downs & suit jackets.

CXXVII.

I think I will always wonder which words of yours were true

& which you coated in honey to make sweeter...

you did know that honey isn't sweet like sugar, right?

CXXVIII.

How could I be upset when you loved me

to the best of your ability?

Love doesn't come in a

"one size fits all."

CXXIX.

You could speak of nothing

& I'd still be happy to

hear the melody of your voice.

CXXX.

I think you've told me you've loved me multiple times without telling me...

don't worry, I get it, those exact words sound daunting.

CXXXI.

I love you in secrecy because I've never been good at sharing.

CXXXII.

I've decided against doing grown-up things today.

Leave a message with my nonexistent assistant.

We'll get back to you in 3-5 business days.

CXXXIII.

You don't dance,

& I don't make music.

I think we make a perfect duo.

CXXXIV.

You cannot be surprised that my love for you exists.

Have you met you?

CXXXV.

We do not punish the moon when she changes.

So, why would we punish each other?

CXXXVI.

How much better life would be

if we stopped sugarcoating everything

& said what needed to be said.

CXXXVII.

I do not know why we ask others to break their walls down,

then shutter when they do.

There is such beauty in vulnerability.

CXXXVIII.

I asked him how many times he's been in love.

"As many times as I've had the privilege of looking at you."

CXXXIX.

I don't think there's a secret to being **in love.**

I think that your soul latches onto another

& whispers how happy it is to be **home.**

CXL.

It is hard, yes.

Because people change & feelings…

well they fade.

Leaving you with memories that either

chill or burn you to your core.

CXLI.

freedom is one of the best gifts you will ever receive in life.

CXLII.

I am not your first, & I may not be your last.

But I am your now.

Be here with me.

CXLIII.

There is a fear in releasing a dreamer into the mayhem of the world.

She might actually change it.

CXLIV.

The right one will make you know that you are the right one.

CXLV.

I didn't know that loving you meant I'd one day lose you.

How do I live without you if I've never had to?

CXLVI.

I'd travel to the Himalayas if it meant one more time with you.

CXLVII.

"Do you know how long I've waited for you?"

"No, but I look forward to a lifetime of hearing about it."

CXLVIII.

I am unsure of what our futures hold.

If it'll be ours or mine & yours.

But I think that's the beauty of life.

It's an adventure.

CXLIX.

There is so much music within silence.

shhhhh.

This is my favorite part.

CL.

There is so much more to life than

these little miscellaneous things we fill our days with.

I hope you choose to create something bigger for yourself.

CLI.

Every day you wake up is another chance.

CLII.

You owe yourself.

You owe yourself the chance to bloom.

CLIII.

I think I'll run out of words one day,

& when that day comes…

I hope you leave a trail of kisses

that'll always hum.

CLIV.

Maybe there isn't gold at the end of the rainbow, after all.

Maybe the end is just the beginning of another start.

CLV.

I want all my love poems to be about you…

I hope you stick around just to see it through.

CLVI.

I revisit the painful parts of life quite often.

How else would I've learned to bloom in the dark?

CLVII.

I don't know if I'm the person they wanted me to be.

But I know I'm the person I needed to be.

CLVIII.

I still see your light when your darkness consumes you.

There is beauty in that, too.

CLIX.

Growing is letting go of the beliefs you've conjured from their thoughts of you.

CLX.

Be real.

Would you have wanted less heartache

If you knew the warrior in you

needed no armor in battle?

CLXI.

I wouldn't ask you to travel the world to see me.

I know you'd do it regardless.

CLXII.

Believe me when I tell you.

I have never met a soul that feels as close to God as yours.

CLXIII.

Why would I worry about tomorrow

when today has just begun?

CLXIV.

potatoes come in all shapes & sizes & are useful at any point of the day.

I'm sorta like a potato.

CLXV.

The amount of infinity necklaces

I've collected from boys who thought

they could handle a woman.

CLXVI.

I poured into you from an empty cup,

thinking that if I filled you

you'd return the favor.

CLXVII.

I never realized I had daddy issues until

I turned to you thinking I'd find my worth.

CLXVIII.

I hate slow walkers.

Don't you understand I have a date with destiny?

CLIX.

It's a Friday night in the summer heat of August.

I'm watching couples holding hands instead of doing so myself.

Maybe Friday night in the fall breeze of September will be different.

CLXX.

There are people in the backgrounds of my pictures.

They all have lives I know nothing about.

I wonder how many times I've been in theirs.

Maybe they wonder about my favorite flower

CLXXI.

I have a love for things I do not know yet.

That is the beauty of mystery.

CLXXII.

Of course your mother still asks about me.

CLXXIII.

I listened to conversations in languages I did not know

& wondered how people could ever hate the music that fell from their
lips.

CLXXIV.

It's amazing what you can accomplish

when you move out of your way.

CLXXV.

I sometimes wish I was born in an era where technology wasn't prevalent.

I'd love to wait in anticipation for your love letters.

CLXXVI.

Forgive me.

I am still learning how to swim in the deep end.

CLXXVII.

I listen to the cadence of your voice when I lose momentum.

CLXXVIII.

If we never end up together,

at least I know our souls are connected.

CLXXIX.

I wonder if we'll ever meet again….

but in the case we don't,

it was a great 2 minutes of getting to know you.

CLXXX.

I kick myself every time I have a crush.

Like, hey.

You know you can be by yourself for a minute or two,

right?

CLXXXI.

You can question it all you'd like.

But what happened, happened the way it should have.

If it could've happened differently, it would've.

CLXXXII.

you're never lost.

sometimes just misplaced.

CLXXXIII.

I think maybe we've met before.

Not here, but in another space of life.

CLXXXIV.

Time has forced me to move on,

but I don't know if I've ever let go.

CLXXXV.

For if we are not each other's here on earth,

I pray we are each other's somewhere in the clouds.

CLXXXVI.

I don't know why we're so scared to live...

as if this life is guaranteed...

humans are the fucking worst.

CLXXXVII.

Repetition is a relative of insanity.

CLXXXVIII.

I will not ask you to stay if you'd much rather leave.

A queen does not beg for the company of a jester.

CLXXXIX.

I make myself sad.

I make myself happy.

I'm self-sufficient that way.

CXC.

I love that you are living your life...

I just wish it was with me.

CXCI.

You don't know my strength, but I do.

I've walked through the fires of hell & remained whole.

CXCII.

We must thank ourselves for shedding the skin of the old us.

CXCIII.

My mother couldn't tame the wild in me.

Why do you think you can?

CXCIV.

Do not mistake the gentle of my fingertips as weakness.

I will squeeze the blood from your heart & paint a new piece.

CXCV.

I stare at the phone...

I know I shouldn't...

waiting for you to call...

you won't...

keep hope alive?

CXCVI.

I do not know how humans live without a Mommom.

Their love is indescribable & unparalleled.

CXCVII.

I know you aren't all the same,

but dammit I'm tired of finding the ones that are.

I'd like to call Gold Fish now.

CXCVIII.

You sent her into the fire & expected her not to burn.

CXCIX.

I'm trying to find the words to convince myself that I don't need you.

Moving on is hard sometimes.

Chapter 23

CC.

I don't know why we want to be loved

by people who do not even like themselves.

CCI.

I called to just tell you that I'm happy you're happy.

I'll leave a voicemail after the beep.

CCII.

we find such peace with sand beneath our feet.

every grain a story of its own.

CCIII.

the sun & the moon share the sky with no complaints.

how awful are humans to feel entitled to things that were never theirs.

CCIV.

I know not where your head is,

but where your heart is...

love requires I know both.

CCV.

the thought that we only have one soulmate is asinine.

human beings are far too complex to only understand the depths of a single soul.

CCVI.

I'd burn in hell with you if it meant

your arms still kept me warm at night.

CCVII.

You were home until you changed the locks & forgot to tell me.

CCVIII.

I got used to not seeing your name light my phone.

Why did you return?

CCIX.

I'd like to align with you the way stars do at night.

Be a sliver of light to guide you through the darkness.

CCX.

I stared from a distance,

admiring the beauty that is you.

If I only ever see you again in my dreams,

I pray they never end.

CCXI.

You have been places I know nothing about & have loved people I do
not know.

Fascinating how life draws strangers together.

CCXII.

The more I watched you from a distance the greater my realization grew...

I never knew the you of you, just someone completely untrue.

CCXIII.

If I throw up my flag & yell, "Forfeit!"

will you release your grip from my heart

& let me breathe?

CCXIV.

One day I won't feel the need to explain my worth.

I'll understand by then that anyone who needs an explanation

is someone I do not need.

CCXV.

Why does everything have to have such depth to be felt?

Can't we just look at the sun & know it burns?

CCXVI.

I wish this was still the early 2000's.

You'd burn me a CD,

label it in gel-pen with our names,

& AIM message me asking if I liked it.

CCXVII.

I don't honestly think that love is overrated...

but I say it to protect the soft edges of an over abused organ.

CCXVIII.

I know love should not hurt.

I wonder when my heart will know that, too.

CCXIX.

It's taken me time to love myself.

Time to understand me

& what I love

& what I want.

I have done a lot of work

renovating the spaces within.

CCXX.

We both know the same person that we both do not know.

CCXXI.

& if all the lights went out in this city we call home,

I know our love will spark a fire.

CCXXII.

You look through me, & for the first time I feel seen.

CCXXIII.

It's almost ironic that the ones who want to

give the most love are the ones who never receive.

CCXXIV.

How lucky are we.

To walk the lands of the earth.

& breathe all her air.

CCXXV.

I do not want to know your favorite color or your favorite song.

I want to know what keeps you up at night.

Where you go when you stare into the distance.

How you keep moving forward when I'd understand if you asked for a break…

CCXXVI.

I've knocked on death's door.

God answered & said, "Try again."

CCXXVII.

I give compliments, though I do not ever wish to receive them.

I just want people to know that I recognize the effort they put into themselves.

Self-love is beautiful.

CCXXVIII.

I prayed for you.

I did.

You were my idea of perfect.

But just that...

an idea.

CCXXIX.

I want to freeze time.

Right here.

Right now.

& bask in the light that is your soul.

CCXXX.

I'd like to be an otter with you one day.

Hold hands & never drift out of each other's sight.

CCXXXI.

Conversations are different at night.

We unmask ourselves & pour truth into the daily lies.

CCXXXII.

If we are right, but this is wrong,

I pray we find each other again in time.

CCXXXIII.

Your eyes they do shine.

With a hope for tomorrow.

Please, keep believing.

CCXXXIV.

I will always have love for the ones who bruised me.

They did not break me.

They reminded me of my resilience.

CCXXXV.

Your words are on loop in my mind.

The smile you give me is stained on my lips.

Your company feels like home.

When I prayed for my person,

I didn't know it was a prayer for

you.

CCXXXVI.

We have never kissed, & yet I taste the warmth of your lips daily.

CCXXXVII.

Here I was, thinking I'm invisible.

I have the attention of humans

I've never had the privilege of properly greeting.

CCXXXVIII.

I keep hoping I'll run into you.

My heart is having a hard time letting go.

CCXXXIX.

I am brilliant, & I will stop minimizing myself

to make others comfortable.

CCXL.

I do not love you because I'm supposed to.

I love you because you deserve to be loved.

you deserve to be cherished.

you deserve.

(Letter to me)

CCXLI.

Forgive yourself for all the times

you've let yourself down.

You will rise again.

CCXLII.

Dandelions remind me that even beauty can grow from chaos.

CCXLIII.

I don't need a promise ring,

just promise to ring.

CCXLIV.

Growing up is for suckers.

Pass me the remote.

Cartoons are on.

CCXLV.

Let it go & watch the world return you tenfold.

CCXLVI.

I'm sure God cries

when He hears the words

you whisper about yourself.

As if He didn't spend hours

pouring all your worth into you.

CCXLVII.

I like you like coffee.

Twice a day.

CCXLVIII.

A love so deep the ocean couldn't grasp it.

CCXLIX.

your lips did not move

& yet I heard you.

CCL.

My Mommom has always told me

that I cannot change people,

but I may change myself if I'd like.

How right she was.

CCLI.

There are times where you'll feel that you gave up on them & let go,

but please remember that you cannot save a soul who doesn't want help.

CCLII.

growth is uncomfortable, but we mistake it for pain.

CCLIII.

-

I looked to you to help with my growth.

You left.

Thank you.

CCLIV.

it's 10:38 AM,

& I'm biting the crap

out of the straw in my cup.

I wish it was your lip instead.

CCLV.

The sun doesn't question

where she'll get the energy to shine.

Neither should you.

CCLVI.

Give me your hand.

I will show you the beauty that is life.

CCLVII.

I won't say that I've never felt this way before because that would be a lie.

& I do not want to lie to you because I love you.

& love & honesty are building blocks to a lasting always…

which is what I want with you.

So, I will say that you reignited a flame in me that I thought was extinguished decades ago.

& if I never get the chance to show you that…

well, I hope you reread these love notes & just somehow know.

CCLVIII.

You have to find peace in knowing

that certain things did not work out in order to protect you.

CCLIX.

I pull away & you pull me closer.

Is this what safe love feels like?

CCLX.

I am surrounded by words every second I exist.

If you dare approach me, have words worth conversing.

CCLXI.

they say love is a drug,

which would make you my handler.

how much do I get for a broken heart?

Chapter 23

CCLXII.

I do not know how long pain lasts.

I do know that every day I continue to breathe

is another chance to heal.

CCLXIII.

But first, a nap.

How else will I spark creativity?

CCLXIV.

You are so much more than a pretty face.

You are the sun & the moon simultaneously,

rising & falling with each script change in the play of life.

CCLXV.

I'd give you my eyes if it meant you'd see how the world cherishes you.

CCLXVI.

She's thorny like a rose bush

Beautiful to look at

But hard to get near.

She allows few to brush

The softness of her petals

To take in the scent of her perfume

To hold her delicacy.

Too many hands have caressed her

Before and the damage is present

On the tips of her fingers

That now look bruised.

Time has taken its toll.

A dozen of her would make

Just one happy

But don't extend your hand

Too far, just yet.

She is protective of her sweetness.

CCLXVII.

The real heroes in life are the ones

who bring light in spite of feeling

consumed by the dark.

CCLXVIII.

It is not your fault they cannot see

the spirit within themselves that you see.

CCLXIX.

You are the ocean, fluid & full of breath.

You expand to give space to all, willingly, even if undeserved.

You crash, then find a calm.

Full of depth that only few may ever reach.

How beautiful are thee.

CCLXX.

I want memories.

Me & you together always.

Let's make it happen.

CCLXXI.

Sometimes you just have to say

"Fuck It"

& go about the day.

CCLXXII.

The sooner people realize that nothing really matters,

the sooner they'll find peace.

CCLXXIII.

I watch older couples repeatedly fall in love.

Tales untold between the creases of their aging flesh.

How long their hearts have touched each other…

impressive.

But, not nearly as impressive as the way

their souls still dance

together.

Chapter 23

CCLXXIV.

If life is a circle,

how do I know if this is the

beginning or the end

of our tragic love affair?

CCLXXV.

I have yet to meet you, but I know that I am already in love with you.

I know that you will be a light for the world who sees too much darkness.

I know that you will create a life full of sunflowers that many will try to pick, but few will be successful.

I love you because you will always be the best piece of me.

CCLXXVI.

But what if love is not enough to keep me lifted?

Will I drown & wish it had been?

CCLXXVII.

Both Da Vinci & Michelangelo spent years completing memorable works of art.

Of course it's taking time to complete you.

CCLXXVIII.

I think it impossible to love you anymore than I do in this moment.

Then I feel your energy in my memories,

& I fall in love all over again.

CCLXXIX.

I watched a little boy's mother open a steel door for him.

Arms high in the air, he came through screaming for joy.

How we forget how beautiful simplicity is.

CCLXXX.

I cannot grasp why you think I need fixing.

When I have never wanted to change you.

Repaint your canvass.

Rearrange your pieces.

I know that there was no mistake in your creation.

Why do you feel there was one in mine?

CCLXXXI.

Do you think that some way, somehow, our souls created a connection on one side of the country despite us being thousands of miles apart on that coast? & then they some way, somehow found each other again on the opposite side of the country ready to connect again?

I swear I have loved you for an eternity.

CCLXXXII.

Often times we hang on because we are scared

to see the after without it being like the before.

We are so used to comfort that change stirs anxiety.

But our guts push us to feel beyond the lining of our hearts.

So, we must hold onto the memories,

but be mindful when we outgrow

the pot we have been planted.

CCLXXXIII.

I can't wait to talk to God.

I hope He has unlimited office hours.

CCLXXXIV.

Be the baby bird.

Jump even if you're unsure you'll fly.

CCLXXXV.

The heart you stole from me,

does it sit in a jar somewhere close to you?

My fingers trace the scar across my chest daily.

CCLXXXVI.

I want a love that both consumes me

& let's me breathe.

One that I struggle to explain because

There aren't actual words to describe the

Magnitude in which my heart longs to feel

Yours.

I want a love that I only question in terms

Of what sauce we're getting with nuggets,

Knowing damn well you'll curse me out after

I purposefully pick the one that you

hate.

I want a love that is spoken without saying it.

One that is passed through your eyes,

Reaching closer to touch your soul.

I want a love that burns long enough

to keep me warm at night

& wakes me with a gentle

Brush to cool.

I want a love that loves my love.

I want a you.

CCLXXXVII.

the day the world stops spinning,

I hope to be in your presence.

if your eyes are the last I see,

I'll be staring at eternity.

CCLXXXVIII.

You cannot cage the wild & expect it to become obedient.

CCLXXXIX.

You painted stars onto the darkness of night

& reminded me that anything is possible.

CCXC.

I watch my Mommom take care of my mother 50 years later.

Everything I know & understand about love begins & ends with her.

I pray that when she leaves the earth, her spirit comes back in the form of my daughter.

So she sees that her lessons never went unnoticed.

CCXCI.

I feel the pains of the world in ways that most do not.

Which is why my heart sings in tunes

of extreme despair traced with a line of sweetness.

I want to believe in the goodness, the wholeness that life form

is supposed to disperse onto the grounds we inhabit.

But my eyes are constant pools when I hear the grievance.

Maybe it's empathy, a piece of me that relates to others.

I'm not sure.

But if I drown in the pools,

at least they'll know I felt it, too.

CCXCII.

Truth is, I know who I am without you, but I love the me I am with you.

You bring out a side of me I do not recognize, a new introduction.

I wonder how you saw her before I did.

You reached past the shallow end, where most stop to dabble...

never fully intrigued to sink deeper...

into areas not yet claimed & planted a seed.

How beautiful is the sun that grew from the flower.

A new beginning.

CCXCIII.

I never cared about being my parents' favorite child

because I knew I was yours.

A grandmother's favor trumps all.

CCXCIV.

I want to love you in every state in the US.

We have 49 more to go...

I hope forever sounds okay to you.

CCXCV.

It isn't hard for me to show you I love you.

It's hard for me to say it.

Not because I don't feel it or think it constantly.

Because I'm unsure my heart could withstand

another scratch.

CCXCVI.

Real love & desire to be with someone will crash through every wave
until the sea calms again.

CCXCVII.

She sees life through a lens you cannot purchase at any shop.

Chapter 23

CCXCVIII.

if it hurts,

it is not love,

but the feeling

of growth

& letting go.

CCXCIX.

Life has no map.

Roam where your heart leads you.

CCC.

I am not perfect.

I have hurt people.

I have broken a heart.

I have lied.

I have wished for something I did not mean.

I have cried over someone who didn't deserve me.

I have yelled at someone who did.

I've wasted what others would appreciate.

I've taken for granted what many don't have.

I've complained.

I am not perfect.

I am human.

That makes me perfectly

imperfect.

CCCI.

You threw me a line even though you knew I could swim.

Your want to protect me warms my entirety.

CCCII.

I think our love could set the world on fire.

together, we can watch it burn from the highest mountain.

CCCIII.

Do you know what makes life beautiful?

Perception.

You & I will never

see life the same,

simply because we were not gifted

with an identical pair of eyes.

The beauty is that we will never truly know

how the world & all her glory appears…

just that we'll wake with the rise of burning rays

& rest with the light of a transitioning satellite.

CCCIV.

I've never had to explain to you

where my mind drifts in the earliest hours of the day.

You were already there, waiting for me to join.

CCCV.

Really, don't worry about it.

In the end, it doesn't matter.

The world stops spinning.

CCCVI.

When I try to think of anything other than you,

I somehow wonder back to the depths of your soul.

It's cliché, I know.

But you intertwine your fingers in mine,

& I feel my heart lean towards yours

in an attempt to become

one.

CCCVII.

One day, you will meet someone. You'll be minding your business, getting things done, & they will appear. Not in a genie in a bottle type of way, but in a way that makes you double-take. You will see them, not just notice their presence, but see their existence. You may wonder of their timing, random in the moment they become visible. But you will meet someone. & their words will fill the spaces in between yours, energy magnetic. It's possible they are your counter, but it's possible they are not all in the same breath.

The lesson is not of soulmates.

It is of appreciating another for their being.

CCCVIII.

I have a kid brother who protects me like an older.

I hope my daughter feels the safety net her brother will create for her.

CCCIX.

You're a part time relationship,

entering & leaving as you please.

You numb my mind

then drag me around.

Scared to lose me,

but I know you're aware

that you couldn't.

You're a seed developed weed

that chokes the air from the flowers of sun,

only to let go momentarily...a faint laughter.

I find the rope to pull me,

but you grip,

white-knuckle bearing.

It is not love,

but your presence is

homely.

I wish we'd let

each other

go.

CCCX.

I've never been good at directions

which is probably why I got lost

in your words and

ignored your actions.

CCCXI.

Oh, darling. I'm an artist.

Of course, I'm not all the way here.

CCCXII.

It's hard not to fall for a girl like you.

Your energy is unmatched.

Just make sure that when they fall,

they fall into all the layers that are you

& not just the surface.

You deserve more than a half love.

CCCXIII.

you're a free spirit with a heart bigger than most

& one that many don't understand,

though they try their best to.

but, sometimes even their best is not enough.

& that's not a reflection of them being a lesser person,

they just can't surpass the boundaries they understand.

CCCXIV.

I sometimes think that most don't know

what real love is

until it slips between their fingers

& ends in grasping air that

lingers with the scent of a past forever.

CCCXV.

I wish I could capture the sound of your smile,

the warmth that radiates between the parentheses.

you have a laugh that lingers,

your soul shining through the spaces of silence.

you are felt before you are ever seen.

If I believed in magic, I'd say you were magical.

But that seems too simple for a complexity such as you.

If eternity exists, we'll know it's your heart.

You are a light that beams without even knowing.

CCCXVI.

Wanna change our names & move to an island?

We can start a life that no one has to know about.

CCCXVII.

My heart breaks for the babygirls

who look in the mirror

& don't recognize their worth.

I was that babygirl at one point.

It is a process,

but I promise the clouds will break

& the sun within you

will shine brighter

than any darkness

that consumes you.

CCCXVIII.

I look forward to the day I pour all of my love into someone,

knowing the floor of my heart will not break & have me fall through.

CCCXIX.

I was given a name far stronger than I ever knew.

I walked on dirt paths & watched as flowers bloomed.

CCCXX.

Why do you settle as someone's second choice

when you know you're worthy of being a priority?

CCCXXI.

Just promise me one thing.

You will never stop being you

because you feel the need to please everyone.

Your happiness matters, too.

CCCXXII.

I have a ring for each finger,

except the one that says "I'm taken."

I'd like to believe that the universe is

still creating the perfect moment

with the perfect ring

to give to the perfect human

who believes I'm perfect

even if we've agreed it's nearly impossible.

CCCXXIII.

It'd be easier if I could drag your name through mud

& crush the life out your soul, as you have done to me.

But I am fortunate in having a heart that understands not

everyone speaks the same love language.

I hope the best for you, truly...

because a lifetime of searching

only to break multitudes seems

an awful long & unhappy journey.

CCCXXIV.

my lifestyle consists of

coffee twice a day,

telling people they're beautiful,

choosing nap time over all,

& crying.

CCCXXV.

if you knew the madness that occurs in the temple of my brain,

you'd either run in fear or

be in awe of the way I compartmentalize the realms of existence.

CCCXXVI.

At 19, my Mommom traveled 6,775 miles to a country that told her she was unworthy because her native tongue was not English.

Her past is coated with bombs dropped by the humans she later coexisted with.

Her life sewn into materials that draped the walls of former, American presidents.

You ask me how I see the light in the darkness of everything.

I was raised by a woman who carried the hatred of the free-world

on her back without complaining.

The scar down her spine speaks volumes.

CCCXXVII.

Anymore love poems & I'll have an entire collection about just you.

CCCXXVIII.

most give up because they feel that

their dreams will never be their reality.

but you are not most.

CCCXXIX.

I watched your last tear fall from your eye & land in your coffee cup.

Your lips touched the edge, a pause before the sip.

I promise the bitterness will not always exist.

CCCXXX.

Cry. Ask for Clarity. Laugh. Move On.

CCCXXXI.

A million stars in the sky

& still I only want to exist

in the universe you've created.

CCCXXXII.

Is a day dream still a day dream

if I dream it all 24 hours of the day?

I just love your memory & want it to stay.

CCCXXXIII.

You could spend twice the amount of years with me

that I've been alive & still not know my entirety.

I am an entire world existing in a single soul.

CCCXXXIV.

If I lose your grip while we're on the sea,

I pray the wind brings you back to me.

I've lived without you once before,

please don't reopen that door.

Days with you are so much better,

like fall & sweaters,

my favorite weather.

.

CCCXXXV.

Humans make life so miserable

then judge the ones who escape reality

& find the fun.

CCCXXXVI.

The scariest part is that

hearts break in silence,

though they're made of glass.

I wish you believed that

we would've last.

CCCXXXVII.

I annoy people because I can still see life

through the eyes of a child.

It is not naïve.

It is knowing of the ugliness the world possesses,

but still choosing to bask in the glory

that others ignore.

CCCXXXVIII.

You must understand that I live in a world I've coated with color,

Unafraid to be the woman that I have finally discovered,

Hiding in the areas of shadows & grey,

I will almost always ask you to play.

To uncover the soul you have masked in fear,

Intimidated by those who never cheer,

For your success or choices or life's weird turns.

When will you finally learn?

That you matter,

You're important,

You're one of a kind.

& anyone who can't see that is obviously blind.

I dare you to live in a world coated with color,

Be unafraid to be that woman you have

rediscovered.

CCCXXXIX.

I bet that if we combined your lyricism with my ability to move,

we'd create a piece worthy of being nominated for all awards.

CCCXL.

You almost always find yourself in the silence of noise.

CCCXLI.

I have tried to divorce depression,

but she's refused to sign the paperwork.

We're separated...temporarily,

because she's a complete bitch

& likely to return.

CCCXLII.

If we all know this life will one day end,

why do we fear living?

CCCXLIII.

True beauty is knowing yours exists

& still reminding others of their own.

Chapter 23

CCCXLIV.

I will be the light house that brings you home

when your soul has lost its compass.

CCCXLV.

It took me forever to realize that all my love letters

"to you" were actually meant for myself.

You left, but the words I wrote still applied.

CCCXLVI.

Please trust me when I tell you I hate running,

but will run until my legs give out

for a chance to cradle the fragility of your heart.

I'll run away with it, but only because I want to spend

a lifetime of playing freeze-tag with you.

Freeze our journey at all the parts we fall in love all over again.

Tag each memory to save in an archive our children will one day find.

CCCXLVII.

We must protect the humans with kind-hearts,

for they are the ones who see

& understand the world most clearly.

CCCXLVIII.

To be the keeper of secrets is an awfully, large load to carry.

Do you think I could rest within your arms for a second?

CCCXLIX.

It is not hard to hide in plain sight.

So many smile, but feel their spirits crumpling.

laugh, but hear silence that was once music escape their lips.

hug, but shiver at the touch of human connection...

because it's felt like a lifetime since

they've related to a soul embodying a human.

You can never be too sure.

CCCL.

We will stop placing reasons into others

& become the reasons ourselves.

Reasons to smile.

Reasons to be happy.

Reasons to want more life.

CCCLI.

It is easy to place my everything into words.

They do not cower & leave me unheard.

How silly to think I could place me within you.

I'm a universe of color & you're just blue.

CCCLII.

I collected lightening bugs in glass jars.

Transparent to admire the light they bring the dark.

When the night falls & the day rises, their life becomes death.

As someone's lightening bug that brightens the dimming,

may they not cage you & kill the life that is your existence.

CCCLIII.

I am a wildfire.

You cannot control the soul meant to burn

for an eternity.

CCCLIV.

We look at demons as reasons to banish darkness from our lives.

But so much of us is grown in the shadows.

CCCLV.

Her strength?

She has many.

But her most memorable is the way she stands in a room

& commands attention by simply being.

Her soul speaks to many,

reminding of their purpose & worth.

She is capable of individualizing among multiples.

CCCLVI.

Do you know how many stories I have not heard?

How many pages I have not been lost in?

How many words have not touched my soul & fed my mind?

We are given far too many books with a timer set for far too little time.

CCCLVII.

I count life in 8s.

Begin each step with a pointed toe.

& chaîné from everything that attempts to

knock me from my center.

CCCLVIII.

you are all of the beautiful things

that grow & develop

from the seeds intended

to enrich the world.

CCCLIX.

you notice your strength when a similar trial is presented

& you win the case by being your own lawyer.

CCCLX.

I want my daughter's favorite bedtime story to be the tale of us.

A musician who played his heart into a rhythm only she could dance to.

CCCLXI.

I whispered my heartache into the night & woke with a rose by my
pillow.

A splash of sun through the closed window, pink petals rest on the linen.

Your love for me screams in unfamiliar keys.

CCCLXII.

My fingers brushed your arm

& you wrapped my body into your entirety.

Under the stars, I saw your soul undress.

The layers of you more beautiful than the last.

It's incredible how stars burn in the darkness,

filling the world with light.

I am lucky you fell out of the sky into my grip.

CCCLXIII.

It is sad knowing that I can love you in the ways that you need to be loved.

That I can feed your soul & set it on fire.

That I can cradle your heart between my fingers without fumbling.

You are so deserving of a love that does not make you question its existence.

But my love is not the love you need.

& I love you enough to tell you.

CCCLXIV.

I bet relationships lasted longer way back when

because cameras were not equipped to capture

the full resolution of a soul.

CCCLXV.

We love beginnings because we know they're a chance to start over.

Perhaps we'll stop starting them on the first days of months

& start instead on a random Wednesday

during the second week of October.

Because beginnings don't have a specific date.

They just begin.

& what better day to begin something than today.

ABOUT THE AUTHOR

I find that "About Me" pages are often quite boring, and I'd like to believe that I'm not that way. So, I'll give you the run down about the most important pieces of me in as little words as possible.

My name is Cheyenne, but I generally go by Chey. I'm not Chey, by the way…not entirely. I'm an East Coast gal at heart, maneuvering my way through the West Coast hills…and let me tell you, life is different over here—different in the most magical way possible. I have a love for the sun and the way she lights the world. I admire the moon and how she changes often, but always lends herself to humans. & I find that the stars at night remind us that we can shine no matter our size.

May your day be ever filled with love, light, and of course, an abundance of chicken tenders.

~Cheyenne Pajardo

Made in the USA
Lexington, KY
01 December 2019